Marc Andreessen and the Development of the Web Browser

Kathleen Tracy

Mitchell Lane
PUBLISHERS

PO Box 619
Bear, Delaware 19701

Unlocking the Secrets of Science

Profiling 20th Century Achievers in Science, Medicine, and Technology

Marc Andreesen and the Development of the Web Browser

· ·

Library of Congress Cataloging-in-Publication Data
Tracy, Kathleen.
   Marc Andreessen and the development of the Web browser/Kathleen Tracy.
     p. cm. — (Unlocking the secrets of science)
   Includes bibliographical references and index.
   Summary: A biography of the computer programmer who, as a college student, developed the first graphical Internet browser, a user-friendly program to better access the World Wide Web.
   ISBN 1-58415-092-0
   1. Andreessen, Marc—juvenile literature. 2. Browsers (Computer programs)—Juvenile literature. 3. Computer programmers—United States—Biography—Juvenile literature. 4. Telecommunications engineers—United States—Biography—Juvenile literature. [1. Andreessen, Marc. 2. Computer programmers. 3. Browsers (Computer programs) 4. Internet. 5. World Wide Web.] I. Title. II. Series.
TK5102.56.A53 T73 2002
005.7'1376—dc21
                                             2001038021

ABOUT THE AUTHOR: Kathleen Tracy has been a journalist for over twenty years. Her writing has been featured in magazines including The Toronto Star's "Star Week," *A&E Biography* magazine, *KidScreen* and *TV Times*. She is also the author of numerous biographies including "The Boy Who Would Be King" (Dutton), "Jerry Seinfeld – The Entire Domain" (Carol Publishing) and "Don Imus – America's Cowboy" (Carroll & Graf). She recently completed "God's Will?" for Sourcebooks.

PHOTO CREDITS: cover: Archive Photos; p. 6 Archive Photos; p. 13 AP Photos; p. 18 AP Photos; p. 24 Archive Photos; p. 30 Hulton Getty; p. 36 AP Photos

PUBLISHER'S NOTE: In selecting those persons to be profiled in this series, we first attempted to identify the most notable accomplishments of the 20th century in science, medicine, and technology. When we were done, we noted a serious deficiency in the inclusion of women. For the greater part of the 20th century science, medicine, and technology were male-dominated fields. In many cases, the contributions of women went unrecognized. Women have tried for years to be included in these areas, and in many cases, women worked side by side with men who took credit for their ideas and discoveries. Even as we move forward into the 21st century, we find women still sadly underrepresented. It is not an oversight, therefore, that we profiled mostly male achievers. Information simply does not exist to include a fair selection of women.

Contents

The small, round Sputnik was the first man-made satellite launched into outer space.

Chapter 1

From Outer Space to Cyber Space

• •

Kids all over the world grow up today using computers and the Internet. They routinely log on to play games, send e-mail to each other, research homework and browse fun sites like Nickelodeon.com and CartoonNetwork.com. But if it wasn't for a little mixed-breed dog named Laika, we might not even have the Internet.

On October 4, 1957, Russia, which was then called the Soviet Union, launched the first man-made satellite into outer space. Called Sputnik, the satellite was very small, only about the size of a basketball, and weighed just over 180 pounds. But it went into orbit around the earth and on that day the Space Age was born.

A month later, on November 3, Sputnik II was launched. This time, the satellite weighed more than half a ton and it carried a passenger—a dog named Laika, which means "barker" in Russian. Laika became the first living Earth creature to blast off into space and orbit the earth. Sadly, scientists at that time didn't know how to get space capsules back to Earth so she died in space. But in a very big way, her sacrifice would eventually lead to the formation of the Internet and pave the way for a young college student named Marc Andreessen to create the software that would make the Internet as useful and popular as it is today.

After the Soviets successfully ushered in the Space Age with their triumphant Sputnik missions, the American government was anxious to catch up and even surpass their achievements. As a result, the Advanced Research

Project Agency, also known as ARPA, was formed. The Agency's job was to develop ways that computers could help to improve all American technology, especially what was needed to compete in what was quickly termed the "Space Race."

The man chosen to spearhead this effort in October 1962 was Dr. J.C.R. Licklider, who once told University of Minnesota researchers William Aspray and Arthur Norberg that "I was interested in a new way of doing things." Dr. Licklider's goal was to figure out a way for people living in different places to communicate with one another by using a computer.

The obvious benefit of this would be that scientists all over the country could work together on a single project, such as launching a manned spacecraft into orbit. So Dr. Licklider hired a group of computer scientists from different universities and asked them to develop such a system, which he jokingly called an "Intergalactic Computer Network." A network in this case referred to the ability of a computer to communicate with other computers by using telephone wires.

It took a total of seven years of research and experimentation, but finally in 1969, the world's first computer network became a reality when a system called ARPANET connected four universities—UCLA, the University of Utah, Stanford and the University of California at Santa Barbara. Each had been among those hired to research and develop the system when ARPA was formed.

From the very beginning, ARPANET was considered a fantastic success. Just as Dr. Licklider dreamed, scientists were able to share data and access other computers thousands of miles away. By 1971, the number of universities and government agencies connected through ARPANET had grown to twenty-three. In 1972, one of the computer scientists working on ARPANET, Robert Kahn, held the first public demonstration of the system at the International Computer Communication Conference. To many people, it seemed like something taken from science fiction.

However, as amazing as ARPANET was for research, the most popular feature quickly became the simple ability to send direct electronic messages from one person to another, which was called e-mail. And as more computers were added to ARPANET, more and more people relied on these "instant letters."

In 1973, ARPANET went international when it established connections with the University College in London, England and the Royal Radar Establishment in Norway. And over the next several years hundreds of "hosts," as each computer on the network is called, were added. Now that ARPANET was a success, the next step was to make it accessible to even more people. But there was a problem—there were many different kinds of computers and like people in different countries who speak different languages, these computers couldn't understand each other.

Among the people who worked to solve this problem was a young computer scientist named Vinton Cerf, who said in an online interview with Planetary.org that "The idea of connecting computers and interacting with them remotely or having them interact with each other was completely captivating. I'm fascinated by finding simple rules that will allow complex systems to interwork."

Assisted by his colleague Robert Kahn, Cerf eventually designed a common computer language, also known as a protocol, that finally enabled Licklider's "Intergalactic Network" to become a reality. Cerf called his new system TCP/IP. That stands for "transmission control protocol" and "Internet protocol." By using the new TCP/IP standards, a kind of coding system that electronically describes data such as the words in this chapter, different computers could understand each other over the network.

The term TCP/IP refers to the two separate parts of the coding system. Every computer that is linked to the Internet understands these two protocols and uses them to send and receive data along the network. This achievement was so important that Vinton Cerf is now known as the Father of the Internet.

Looking back today, Cerf is humble about his feat, and said to Planetary.org, "I think creativity is simply a matter of avidly putting together ideas that don't necessarily go together at first."

Once TCP/IP was accepted as the standard computer language, a new term was coined to describe the collection of hosts on ARPANET—the Internet. The word was meant to describe the way these computer networks were connected together throughout the world.

By 1984, there were over 1000 Internet hosts around the world and more of the public was using computers, particularly students at universities and colleges, many who logged on just to use e-mail. Businesses were also interested in the Internet as a way to communicate with each other and with their clients and customers. But these first computers were very different from what we have in our homes today. They were still on the bulky side.

The Internet became even more popular not long afterward with the development of what were called "personal computers," also known as PCs. These were machines that were small enough to sit on a desk and just as important, they were affordable for most people.

But the Internet still had one drawback. What you saw on the computer screen was only text, or written words. At that time there was no way to send pictures or graphics over the Internet. It would take a young computer genius from the Midwest to solve that problem and literally change history.

Internet pioneer, Marc Andreessen

Chapter 2

Computer Whiz Kid

Marc Andreessen was born on July 9, 1971 in Cedar Falls, Iowa. When Marc was still a toddler, his family moved to New Lisbon, Wisconsin, so his dad Lowell could work for an agricultural seed company called Pioneer Hi-Bred International. New Lisbon is a small town with a population of less than 2,000 people located two and a half hours north of Milwaukee. Three years after Marc's birth, Marc's younger brother Jeff was born.

Like a lot of kids who grow up in small towns, Marc sometimes found New Lisbon frustrating because there never seemed to be enough to do. But while other boys his age played sports or got into mischief, Marc would spend hours taking things apart to see how they worked.

Although neither of his parents were particularly technology minded—his dad was a district sales manager for Pioneer and his mom Patricia worked for Land's End, the clothes catalog company—Marc soon found himself drawn to computers.

"He's been in computers ever since he was a small boy," Lowell Andreessen recalled to Lee Hawkins, Jr. of the *Wisconsin State Journal*. But because personal computers (PCs) were still a new technology, Andreessen's school didn't have one. So his parents got one for him when he was in the seventh grade.

"I think we bought him his first computer, a TRS-80, from Radio Shack," Marc's father told Hawkins. "They were just cheap little things, not more than $200 or $300."

Even if he and Marc's mother themselves didn't particularly understand computers, Mr. Andreessen added that "We followed his interests and tried to make it available to him."

Marc's dad also believes the biggest credit for helping his son grow into a computer whiz should go to the local libraries. Marc spent hour after hour reading library books about computers and programming, which was then a relatively new science. He quickly learned how to write basic computer programs and practiced for hours on his computer at home. Programming soon seemed almost as natural to him as breathing.

"I'm a child of the PC revolution," Marc Andreessen told Elizabeth Sikorovsky in an online interview with FCW.com. "I always thought it was really cool back in the 1980s that you could just buy a PC. I grew up with PCs."

But as bright as Marc obviously was, his school grades weren't always as good as his parents might have hoped for or expected. Although he was smart enough to do exceptionally well in school, he couldn't seem to tear himself away from his computer long enough to study his school subjects.

"Marc was a good student, but I'm sure that he could have studied harder to get better grades," Mr. Andreessen admitted to Hawkins. "But computers were his first love." Even so, neither of Marc's parents dreamed their son would one day be known as a famous computer genius. "There were certainly a lot of students in his class who were just as bright or brighter than he was," his father added.

After Marc graduated from high school in 1989, he was accepted as a student at the University of Illinois at Urbana-Champaign.

This was an exciting time in the world of computers, because the Internet had amassed over one million hosts and would soon benefit from two important events.

The first of these happened at the University of Minnesota in 1991. A team of computer programmers, led by Mark McCahill, created Gopher, the first simple, easy-to-understand "point-and-click" navigation system for the Internet. In a press conference, McCahill called it "the first Internet application my mom can use." Gopher was offered free so that everyone using the Internet could access files more easily without needing any special training.

That same year also saw the creation of the World Wide Web by a British researcher named Tim Berners-Lee, who at the time was working at the Particle Physics Laboratory for the European Council for Nuclear Research (CERN) in Geneva, Switzerland. Interestingly, his parents were mathematicians who worked to develop the first commercial computer ever sold. As a child, Berners-Lee's passion was electronics, so when it came time to go to college, he majored in physics.

After he graduated from Oxford University in England, he worked as an independent software consultant before taking the job with CERN. While he was there, Berners-Lee's intention was just to come up with a system that would enable physicists to trade information presented in word, sound and image.

"The original goal was working together with others," he explained to Robert Wright of *Time* magazine. "I thought, look, it would be so much easier if everybody asking me questions all the time could just read my database, and it would be so much nicer if I could find out what these guys are doing by just jumping into a similar database of information for them."

Instead, he revolutionized the Internet by developing three standards called HyperText Markup Language (HTML), the HyperText Transfer Protocol (also known as HTTP, the code via which sites are moved into and out of the Web via "links") and what is now known as the Uniform Resource Locater (URL, which identifies each "packet" of information and gives it its own unique "Internet address"). From these standards, Berners-Lee created the World Wide Web program for the Internet. "It allowed information which was only on the mainframe to be accessed from other platforms," Berners-Lee said in an interview published on ora.com.

Originally, Berners-Lee's program, which he called Enquire, was written to store information between generally unrelated items by using links. But in practical terms, what the program did was enable people using the Internet to combine words, pictures, and sounds on individual pages on the World Wide Web. One of the first pages Berners-Lee put up was the CERN phone book, which, he laughs, "left a lot of community people at CERN thinking that the World Wide Web was a rather strange phone book program."

But Lee told Wright of *Time*, that to him, "The Web was supposed to be a creative tool, an expressive tool."

And that's exactly what happened. In a short time, people began using his standards for personal use, such as putting up Web sites that contained anything from baby pictures to salutes for their favorite celebrities. Nobody was more surprised than Berners-Lee. "I was surprised that people were prepared to write HTML," he says on ora.com, referring to the code in which Web sites are written.

Today, Berners-Lee says he sees the Web as the place where people get to be "intercreative," which he defines as "building together, being creative together.

"People need a balance so society can work out. I believe this is programmed into people, that people feel fundamentally uncomfortable unless they have a balance. The Web has to be sufficiently flexible for that. You have to have a Web which allows the family photograph album to link up to the group picnic to link to the corporate home page."

Looking back on his creation, Berners-Lee is humble. "I happened to be in the right place at the right time, and I happened to have the right combination of background," he said in *Time* magazine. He also added that his accomplishment is "a lesson for all dreamers—that you can have a dream and it can come true."

And it was Berners-Lee's World Wide Web creation that caused Marc Andreessen to dream his own dream.

Tim Berners-Lee created the World Wide Web so people could be more creative with the Internet.

Chapter Three

Putting Together a Mosaic

• •

Besides wanting to know everything he could about computers, Marc Andreessen had another strong desire as a teenager—to leave his small town of New Lisbon and see more of the world. Compared to where he grew up, the University of Illinois at Urbana-Champaign seemed like a huge city, with everybody studying some kind of interesting field. But college wasn't just the chance to learn, it also provided Marc's first exposure to other people who shared his interests and who were as passionate about computers as he was.

Marc said in a Smithsonian Online interview with David Allison that when he enrolled at UIUC, he had no idea what career he was going to pursue, but joked that he was "pretty sure I wasn't going to be a farmer."

For a while he considered electrical engineering because "electrical engineers got paid on average the most in the field," but eventually decided on computer science instead because, he kidded again, "it required the least amount of work."

But in truth Marc wanted to work in computers as a way to help people. "I was considerably more interested in applied programming," he said to Allison, "in actually doing things that people found useful as opposed to just studying theory."

Like a lot of students, Marc also wanted to make some extra money so he looked for a part-time job at the university's National Center for Supercomputing Applications (NCSA), the campus physics research facility.

Andreessen started working in a NCSA research lab and told Allison of Smithsonian Online, "This was really an educational experience because it introduced me to both the world of high-end computing and networking. The Internet was already there; everybody used it because it was there."

Marc also worked for a while at IBM, a company famous for making some of the most popular personal computers. He spent parts of 1990 and 1991 in an IBM co-op program in Austin, Texas which provided him with some great experiences in the computer industry.

Back at the NCSA lab, Marc's job was to write software programs. The pay was $6.85 an hour. But after Tim Berners-Lee introduced the World Wide Web, an idea began to form in Marc's head. Although the Internet and the Web were amazing ways to find information and communicate with other people, Andreessen felt they still weren't living up to their potential.

"The whole Internet phenomenon had been gaining momentum for the past decade, but it was still very much limited to a small audience of people," he told Smithsonian Online's Allison. "It was limited to skilled programmers, for example, and it wasn't friendly enough for people who wanted to do interesting things.

"Networking had arrived so fast, and everything was happening so rapidly, that people just hadn't yet gotten around to making it accessible. So it was primed for someone to come along and try to take all this information and this great networking and pull it together with a graphical interface for the desktop."

So in November of 1992 he approached Eric Bina, one of his friends who also worked at NCSA, and asked if he would like to work on a project with him. Marc wanted to write a user-friendly program to better access the Web, a program that would make browsing the Internet really fun—and be useful, too.

"One idea was that multi-media should be a key part of the Internet," Andreessen told David Allison. "Everyone knew desktop computers and the network were perfectly capable of handling images. The new part was simply combining this idea with the ability to link together resources across the globe.

"I figured out that this was something that we should do and it was the right time and place to do it, and then it was a fairly simple application of just pulling the two halves together."

Bina readily agreed and in their spare time, at nights and during weekends, they collaborated on making Marc's dream come to life.

Although Marc devoted all his time and attention to his own project, he was actually supposed to be writing some 3D software for scientific visualization for NCSA. But instead of being angry or ordering him to stop, the University encouraged Marc.

"I guess you've got to understand the context of what NCSA is," he explained to Thom Stark in an online interview. "It's a fairly free-form environment and we were in an environment where we were able to go do interesting things.

"I mean, NCSA is not a place where there are necessarily a whole lot of well-defined directions or goals. In fact, most of the interesting things that have happened there have been because one or more people decided to do something interesting—and then did it!"

Working many times in the University's old Oil Chemistry Building, Marc and Eric began to write the program that would eventually become known as Mosaic. Four other students helped, too. All of them were so intent on their work that they often wouldn't even leave the building to eat. Instead, they ordered in pizzas and stayed up all night.

Years later, Andreessen would recall those days fondly to the members of the National Press Club. "While we were at the University of Illinois writing Mosaic, working late nights, writing lots of code, we'd download these huge 10-megabyte audio files and listen to National Press Club talks," he said.

"Now, what's kind of funny about that, is that in order to do this we would use our high speed T3 network link which cost about $60,000 a month. We would feed that into a state-of-the-art campus network that cost about $100 million to build. And then play the audio files on a $35,000 silicon graphics workstation. All instead of just turning on the radio or the TV set."

Marc finished by joking, "It really shows the length that computer people will go to, to amuse themselves in the middle of the night while they're working and wondering why they don't have a life."

The first version of Marc's Mosaic browser took him, Eric and the others who pitched in about three months to complete. When they were done they had written a program prototype, or original model, that offered people an easy-to-use method of navigating the Internet.

Although earlier computer browsers allowed users to view pictures on their screens, they could only be opened as separate files. Mosaic allowed images and text to appear for the first time on the same page. It was also much easier to scroll through text. And the introduction of hyper-links allowed users to simply click on a link (usually a different-colored word or words that are underlined) to move to another document, rather than typing in complicated reference numbers.

The importance of Mosaic was huge. With the ability to display colorful graphics and a simple point-and-click interface for finding, viewing, and downloading data over the Web, the Mosaic software made the Internet widely accessible for the first time beyond the scientific branches of universities and the government where it started.

"We literally stole from as many sources as we could find," smiles Andreessen. "And made sure we supported them all. At that time there were twenty or thirty servers supporting hypertext markup language. We made sure that we supported all of those because we thought [it] would be important ... to cover all the bases."

What Marc had created was the world's first graphical Internet browser—and it would be an instant success.

Marc Andreessen led a team of fellow college students to create Mosaic, the world's first graphical Internet browser.

Chapter Four

Starting Over

● ●

Now that Marc Andreessen had created the first graphical Internet browser, the next question was what to do with it. For Marc, there was a simple answer— give it away! Not everybody agreed with him.

"I was skeptical," co-creator Eric Bina told Julie Schmit of *USA Today.* "But it took off like nobody believed."

Initially, only about a dozen people were given the program to try out. Then in 1993, the university made the Mosaic program available free of charge on the Internet.

"We expected that quite a few people would use it. We just tried to hurry and get it out there," Andreessen told David Allison of Smithsonian Online.

Not even Marc could have imagined the response. Within one year, over two million copies had been downloaded by Internet users all around the world. As a result, traffic on the Internet, meaning the number of people logged on, increased by an astonishing 341,634%.

To all of those people, Marc Andreessen became a hero. But to him, it was simply a matter of sharing what he felt belonged to everyone anyway.

"The great thing about the Internet, the thing that catalyzed it in the first place and renews it every day," he pointed out to Allison, "is that there are so many people able to use it, able to do a million different things. It's an open platform and a lot of people are able to apply their energy, and see it bear fruit." Which is why, he said, "We wanted to make Mosaic friendly for people to use."

While the success of Mosaic was fulfilling on a personal level, Andreessen couldn't help but wonder if it might not somehow also turn into a career opportunity. Marc had talked over the possibility of turning Mosaic into a commercial business with Larry Smarr, the director of NCSA, only to be told that was highly unlikely.

Smarr explained to Marc that because NCSA was part of a research institution, they did not have a system in place to start commercial companies. Instead, the University would license out the technology, meaning that other companies would pay the University money to use Mosaic. Many did and soon Mosaic was making money— but not for Marc or the others who worked on it.

Nor would the University try to improve on Marc's program. As he explained to Thom Stark, NCSA "simply wasn't a software development environment. And more to the point, it wasn't a company—it is a research environment. So, as a result it wasn't managed in a way to create and maintain great software." So even though Mosaic had become incredibly popular, "there's basically no way for an organization of that nature to maintain it."

Understanding that his future didn't seem to lay in creating a business with the University using Mosaic, Andreessen realized "it was pretty much knowing that I had to leave there. We basically reached the end of what we were able to do at NCSA. You can only soak up government money for so long trying to do things that the management of the institution really would prefer that you not do."

So after graduating from college, Andreessen knew it was time to leave Mosaic behind and try to find another project that would be as interesting, fun and useful. Even so, part of Marc knew it would be hard. But because of the success of Mosaic, Marc had many job opportunities to choose from. Of all the companies wanting to hire him, he decided to accept a job from a company called Terisa Systems, located in Los Altos, California, near San Francisco.

"I got a really good offer and I think there are some really great people there," Marc told Stark during his online interview. Beyond enjoying the people he worked with, Andreessen was thrilled to be in California. "I fell in love with California the first time I came out here," he added.

Marc described the company he worked for as another research kind of organization financed, as it turns out, by the Advanced Research Projects Agency—ARPA—the agency that paved the way for the Internet in the first place. Marc felt as if he had come full circle in a way.

Although he liked his job at Terisa Systems, he longed to be more creative. Because the company was geared for research, "it wasn't really the sort of environment where you're going to do a whole lot of mainstream software development," he explained to Stark.

But as it turns out, Marc wouldn't be at Terisa Systems for long. He had only been working there for a few months when he received an intriguing e-mail from a man named Jim Clark. Among people in the computer world, Clark was a very famous man.

When he was an associate professor at Stanford University, Clark, along with six graduate students, formed a company called Silicon Graphics, often called SGI. Clark was interested in creating a computer chip that would speed up a computer's ability to display 3D graphics. SGI would go on to supply chips to video game companies such as Nintendo and it also became one of the world's most successful computer-related companies.

What made Clark's success even more amazing is that when he was seventeen years old, he dropped out of school to join the Navy. Once his tour of duty was over, he went back to high school and not only graduated but eventually earned a Master of Science degree in physics from Louisiana State University in New Orleans. Three years later he received a Ph.D. in computer science from the University of Utah.

Although he enjoyed founding Silicon Graphics, Clark got restless once the company became successful. He admitted to friends that being the chairman of a company simply wasn't very much fun so he resigned in 1994. He had decided he would turn his energies toward forming a new company, but this time he wanted to create software.

At first, Clark thought it might be a good idea to work on software that would provide interactive television services, where, for example, people could play along with their favorite game show at home through remote control.

But Clark decided the technology for interactive television was too far away. He wanted to work on something that was useful right away. When he thought about it, he realized the biggest area for opportunity was the Internet.

And when Jim Clark read about Marc Andreessen's Mosaic browser, he knew immediately who he wanted as his new partner and what the company should be.

Jim Clark worked with Andreessen to create a newer, improved version of Mosaic they called Navigator.

Chapter Five
A Second Chance

• •

To Jim Clark, what made the Internet so exciting was the fact that literally millions of new people were logging on every year. He knew that each one of them was a potential customer for software that made the experience of the Internet more fun. It was obvious that Marc Andreessen had created such a software program.

So on the same morning in February, 1994 that Clark resigned from SGI, he sent Marc an e-mail and asked if they could meet. "You may not know me," the e-mail read. "But I'm the founder of Silicon Graphics. I've resigned and intend to form a new company. Would you be interested in getting together to talk?"

Anyone who worked in the computer business knew who Jim Clark was so when Marc received the invitation, he was very excited and immediately accepted. Clark lived in Mountain View, California, not far from where Marc worked at Terisa Systems, so the two men met at a local café.

Marc and Jim spent the next two months getting to know one another and talking about what kind of software project they could work on together that would be useful for the Internet. For Marc, the timing couldn't have been better. Although he liked his current job, he would have been much happier if he was back creating software.

"I like being in a situation where you've got a clear motivation and a clear means to be able to do something really significant," he told Thom Stark.

Finally, Clark offered to pay Marc if he could come up with the right idea. That's when Andreessen suggested a "Mosaic-killer." In other words, a browser like Mosaic but only better.

Clark told David Bottoms of *Industry Week* that Andreessen also suggested that this time around he would not make the same mistakes he had made on Mosaic and he would do it better than he had before. Marc wanted to hire the people who had worked with him before on Mosaic and together they would start from scratch and make the browser more powerful and more useful to people surfing the Internet.

And this time, Marc believed they could build a business around their new browser.

Clark went on to admit to Bottoms, "It seemed a little crazy. No one thought you could build a business around the Internet, but my instincts were if there were 25 million people using it, there was a business to be built."

Marc and Jim's goal was to create *the* Internet software company. Two days after agreeing to go forward with the "Mosaic-killer," Andreessen and Clark flew to Illinois and recruited seven of Marc's former associates to be their first employees. To support the new company, which they named Mosaic Communications Corporation, Clark found an investor who was willing to give them $4 million.

However, when the University of Illinois found out what Marc was doing, a problem developed. According to the rules of the University, anything created by someone who had been enrolled as a student belonged to the University. In other words, even though Marc thought of and created the Mosaic browser, he did not own it.

More than that, the University wanted Marc and Jim to pay them for each browser downloaded if they went ahead with the project. If these disagreements couldn't be resolved, Marc's new dream would be ruined. In the end Clark had to sue the University and eventually the dispute was settled, although Marc and Jim could not use the name "Mosaic" for their new, improved browser. Instead, they named their new company Netscape.

At the press conference where they announced their new company to reporters, Marc—who is 6'4" with a youthful looking face—talked about why it was so exciting to form a new company. "There's something about a start-up," he told Andy Goldberg of *The Daily Telegraph.* "You can basically define the way the world ought to be. Maybe you'll succeed, maybe you'll fail. But you know it's totally up to you."

The software was finished by December, 1994 and just as he had with Mosaic, Marc and Jim agreed to give away their improved browser, which they named Navigator, free on the Internet. Once again, many experts in the computer industry thought their decision would ruin their company. Clark and Andreessen believed differently.

"People knew then that I was certifiably nuts— starting this company, hiring a bunch of students, and now giving the software away," Clark told David Bottoms of *Industry Week.*

Even though they wouldn't make any money on Navigators from people using it on the Web, Marc's company would make money from the software they were developing that would help companies put their Web pages online, so he never worried about money.

But soon enough, Marc, whose official title was Vice President of Technology, would make more money than he ever dreamed anyone could earn when he and Jim decided to make Netscape a public company. In other words, they would offer stock to the public, so that anyone who wanted to could own, or share, a little piece of the company. The more money Netscape made, the higher the value of the stock would go.

In August 1994, Netscape made the first stock—3.5 million shares—available to the public. Because so many people wanted to buy the stock, their demand kept pushing its price higher and higher. By the end of the day, Marc learned he was suddenly worth more than $58 million! At the time, it was hard for him to understand how rich he was.

"It's all still funny money," he told James Collins of *Time.* Because of that, Marc didn't feel rich—he still felt like the same guy he had always been. In fact, Marc didn't let his newfound wealth change him at all.

Instead of going out and buying a huge mansion, Marc continued to live in a rented two-bedroom house filled with books and records and computers and bulldog toys— not expensive art and sculpture. He still went into work every day, getting to the office around 10:00 in the morning and going home at 5:00 p.m. to walk his dog. Marc, who says he doesn't sleep very much, admits he would frequently stay up very, very late working—often until 3:00 in the morning. That's when he would answer his e-mail and think about the future of Netscape.

"On top of that," he told *People* magazine. "I spend half an hour a day reading the news—industry news, world news, U.S. news, business news, and so on. I read CNN, *Wall Street Journal*—all these things online. Sometimes I use it for recreation. Sometimes I use it to look up information on products, sometimes to look at what our competitors are doing."

If there were any doubts that Marc wasn't going to let success change him or give him a big head, listen to how he spent the day he became a multi-millionaire. "I was at home in bed," he told James Collins of *Time*. "I had been up until, like, 3:00 in the morning working, so I woke up at 11:00, logged into my computer from home..." and he says his eyes popped open. But then, he said, "I went back to sleep."

Marc's old friend Eric Bina says Marc was finally living the life he always dreamed about. "He always wanted a job in which he'd be locked in a room with all the newspapers, magazines and access to the networks."

And all his reading made it clear that the two browsers Marc created had changed the world forever.

Marc's latest venture is a company called Loudcloud. Andreessen's dream is to make going to the store to buy software a thing of the past. Instead, he foresees the day when his company will provide software programs people can download directly from the Loudcloud web site for a small fee.

Chapter Six
A New Technological Era

. . . .

In the first year following the release of Navigator, over eight million copies were downloaded off the Internet, making Netscape.com one of the most visited sites on the Web.

But Marc and Jim weren't satisfied with just being popular. They wanted Netscape to be successful, too, so they also created other applications that helped companies make their Web pages safe from hackers, who are people who break into systems to either destroy or steal information.

One way that Marc's company was unique is that in a sense, it only existed online. You couldn't go to the Netscape store—all of their business was provided solely online. That innovation set the stage for other "virtual" companies, meaning they only existed on the web, such as amazon.com, eBay.com and Yahoo.com.

Netscape also collaborated with other companies. Their partnership with Sun Microsystems helped develop JavaScript, an application that allows anyone to create interactive Web sites. As he always had done, Marc was interested in making the Web accessible to everyone, not just computer programmers and scientists.

By June 1996, Netscape estimated that 38 million people were using Navigator. But that kind of success can cause other companies to try and compete. In particular a company named Microsoft wanted a browser of their own to challenge Navigator.

Microsoft was founded by Bill Gates and Paul Allen, who went on to make their company the most powerful computer company in the world. The Windows operating system they developed that ran computers was used in almost every computer bought by the public. Microsoft became so successful that Bill Gates was the richest man in the world.

But it wasn't until Navigator became so popular that Gates began to pay more attention to the Internet. Interestingly, Microsoft paid the University of Illinois to use the Mosaic browser Marc had created, and then used it as a model to create its own browser, called Internet Explorer. Just as Marc had given away Navigator for free, Microsoft included Internet Explorer for free with its other software, such as Windows. Then the company got computer manufacturers to put Internet Explorer on their computers, again giving it away for free.

Because of Microsoft's aggressive tactics, the percentage of computer owners using Navigator began to decline. Just as he had done at SGI, Jim Clark felt it was time to move on to his next project so when America Online offered to buy Netscape, the decision was made to sell. In November 1998, Netscape was bought by AOL and the following March Marc was given the new job of AOL's Chief Technology Officer.

However, even though Microsoft had seemingly won what became known as "the browser wars," Marc felt they had done so by cheating. So Netscape accused Microsoft of unfair business practices and filed complaints with a number of government agencies. Although it didn't save the company from being sold to AOL, it did eventually cause the U.S. Department of Justice to investigate Microsoft.

But back in 1999, Marc was simply trying to adjust to his new job and his new home. When he took the AOL position, he bought a house in Virginia, which he shared with three pet bulldogs. During the day he would surf the Internet and try to always know what new innovations for the Web were being worked on.

"My goal is to know about everything before it happens," he told Shannon Henry of *The Washington Post.* In his first months at AOL, Andreessen said he thought he preferred his new job rather than the one he held at Netscape.

"I don't have a particularly burning desire to run a company," he commented to Henry. "It's not clear I have the temperament for that. I like a job where I can take time, thinking, reading and writing."

However, it wasn't long before Marc got restless and in September 1999, AOL announced he was stepping down. But he wasn't quitting the Internet. Instead, Marc had come up with a new idea for a company. Called Loudcloud, the firm assists other companies to set up Web sites and services. Loudcloud also manages the site.

"If we knock it out of the park, we could radically lower the barrier for Internet start-ups," Andreessen explained to Swartz of *USA Today.* "That would result in more online businesses and greater global expansion for existing Internet companies."

What strikes people about Marc is that even though he works very long hours—14 hour workdays are common—and is a very smart businessman, he is also easy-going and funny, and loves to tell jokes. In other words, he is obviously a man who enjoys the work he does.

"He was a dynamic, energetic figure who could reinforce the spirit of employees," Alex Edelstein, former Navigator product manager, described to Swartz. "He was like a jolt of caffeine."

When Marc Andreessen came up with the idea for a graphical browser, he simply wanted to make surfing the Web a more fun experience. What he didn't realize is how our fascination with the Internet, and the way information can be transmitted and seen thanks to his browser, would in turn change our daily lives forever.

One change is that more and more people "telecommute" over the Internet, meaning they work from home but are still able to work with people at the office. And thanks to telecommuting, it doesn't matter if the office is next door or across the country—communication is instant.

Students can find limitless information on the Internet and doctors can consult with other medical specialists thousands of miles away about the health of a patient. As today's children grow up being accustomed to communicating, researching, playing and interacting with others through the Internet, computers will become an increasingly important part of peoples' lives

But to Marc, all the ways his browser have helped improve our lives are just the beginning. His vision for the future is just as ambitious as his success with Netscape Navigator. Andreessen sees a day when people won't go to the store and buy software in boxes. Instead, they will download programs and other services directly from the Internet through companies like Loudcloud for an inexpensive monthly fee. That way his company is successful and people using the Internet get all the programs they need for a reasonable price.

Whether that new dream comes true or not, Marc is sure to keep creating and thinking of innovative ideas because to him, if you can think it, you can achieve it. And as his friend Quincy Smith, a former Netscape executive, explained to Jon Swartz of *USA Today.* "He's always forward thinking. He does not live in the past."

Marc Andreessen Chronology

- 1971, born July 9 in Cedar Falls, Iowa.
- 1980, receives first computer as gift from parents.
- 1989, enters University of Illinois at Urbana-Champaign.
- 1992, creates the Mosaic graphical browser with six other students.
- 1993, graduates from University of Illinois at Urbana-Champaign with a B.A. in computer science.
- 1994, co-founds Netscape Communications with Jim Clark.
- 1994, named one of the top fifty people under the age of 40 by *Time* magazine.
- 1994, wins an IW Technology of the Year Award for Mosaic.
- 1995, becomes worth $58 million as Netscape becomes a public company and sells stock.
- 1998, sells Netscape to America Online and becomes Chief Technical Officer.
- 2000, co-founds Loudcloud.com.

Web Browser Timeline

- **1957:** Soviet Union launches Sputnik, the first man-made satellite, into space.
- **1958:** In response to the launch of Sputnik, the US Department of Defense establishes the Advanced Research Projects Agency (ARPA), in part to research ways computers could be used to help the US catch up to Soviet military technology.
- **1962:** The RAND Corporation begins research on developing a communication network for military use.
- **1962:** The idea of the Internet is first thought of by the Department of Defense's Advanced Research Project Agency, known as ARPA.
- **1963:** Doug Engelbart invents the *X-Y Position Indicator for a Display System*, or, as it's known today, the mouse.

- **1966:** ARPA receives funding for a computer networking experiment that ties together a number of universities the agency is funding.
- **1969:** The ARPANET network is created, meant to be used by computer scientists as a way to share information with each other. The first four universities to be connected are Stanford, UCLA, UC Santa Barbara and the University of Utah.
- **1971:** Now 23 universities and government research centers are connected. E-mail begins to be one of the most popular features of ARPANET among researchers as a way to share information.
- **1971:** Marc Andreessen is born.
- **1973:** ARPANET adds foreign hosts in England and Norway.
- **1974:** Telenet is formed, the first commercial version of ARPANET intended for the general public.
- **1974:** Vinton Cerf and Robert Kahn establish the Transmission Control Protocol (TCP) and coin the term "Internet."
- **1976:** Queen Elizabeth of England goes online and sends the first royal e-mail.
- **1979:** Students from Duke University and the University of North Carolina establish the first Usenet newsgroups. Users from all over the world join these discussion groups to talk about music, politics, movies and thousands of other subjects.
- **1983:** TCP/IP, created by Vinton Cerf, becomes the universal language of all Internet computers.
- **1983:** The Internet as we know it today is born when ARPANET is split into military and civilian sections.
- **1984:** Author William Gibson coins the term *cyberspace* in his novel, *Neuromancer*.
- **1985:** E-mail is now used widely at many college campuses.
- **1987:** The number of Internet hosts exceeds 10,000.
- **1988:** The first Internet virus, called the Internet Worm, temporarily disables over 5,000 of the available 60,000 Internet hosts.
- **1989:** The number of Internet hosts exceeds the 100,000 mark.
- **1990:** ARPANET is shut down but leaves behind the Internet, now a vast network-of-networks with more than 300,000 hosts.

- **1991:** Computer programmer Mark MacCahill invents Gopher, the first "point-and-click" way to browse files on the Internet.

- **1991:** The World Wide Web is established when Tim Berners-Lee creates the first Web server at the CERN laboratory in Geneva, Switzerland. His computer code shows how words, pictures, and sounds can be combined on Web pages.

- **1993:** Companies are allowed to sell goods and services on the Internet, opening the way for e-commerce.

- **1993:** Marc Andreessen and a group of student programmers develop a graphical browser for the World Wide Web called Mosaic and traffic on the Internet undergoes a huge increase.

- **1994:** Marc Andreessen and Jim Clark form Netscape Communications Corp. Pizza Hut accepts orders for a mushroom, pepperoni with extra cheese over the net.

- **1995:** A team of programmers at Sun Microsystems release an Internet programming language called Java, which radically alters the way applications and information can be retrieved, displayed, and used over the Internet.

- **1996:** The Internet celebrates its 25th birthday. Approximately 40 million people are connected to the Internet and consumers spend more than $1 billion per year on Internet-related goods and services.

- **2000:** The 10,000,000th domain name is registered.

For Further Reading

Books

Marc Andreessen: Web Warrior (Techies)
> by Daniel Ehrenhaft (Twenty First Century Books)

Get on the Net: Everything You Need to Know About the Internet, Including the World Wide Web and Addresses for Hundreds of Fun and Useful Sites.
> by Robert Pondiscio (Morrow/Avon Books)

Nerds 2.0.1: A Brief History of the Internet
> by Stephen Segaller (TV Books, Inc)

History of the Internet: A Chronology, 1843 to the Present
    by Christos J. P. Moschovitis, Hilary Poole, Tami Schuyler,
    Theresa M. Senft (ABC-Clio, Inc.)
*The History of the Internet and the World Wide Web (The Internet
    Library)* by Art Wolinsky (Enslow Publishers)

Magazines

Collins, James, "High Stakes Winners: Meet the Get-Incredibly-
    Rich-Quick Crowd," *Time*. February 19, 1996.

Dunlap, Charlotte, "The Top 25 Executives: Marc Andreessen No.
    8," *Computer Reseller News*. November 13, 1995.

Guthrie, Julian, "The Internet Kid," *The San Francisco Examiner*.
    September 17, 1995.

Holzinger, Albert G., "Netscape Founder Points, and it Clicks,"
    Nation's Business. January, 1966.

Markoff, John, "6 Tips on How to Earn $52 Million by Age 24," *The
    New York Times*. August 14, 1995.

Moeller, Michael, "Netscape's Communication Corp's Vice-
    President of Technology, Marc Andreessen: Interview," *PC
    Week*. Vol. 12, No. 38, September 25, 1995.

Parets, Robyn Taylor, "Netscape's Marc Andreessen," *Investor's
    Business Daily*. January 16, 1996.

Tetzeli, Rick, "What It's Really Like to be Marc Andreessen,"
    Fortune. December 9, 1996.

Wagner, Douglas, "Netscape," *Jones Telecommunications and
    Multimedia Encyclopedia*. Jones International, 1997.

Web Sites

15 Minutes with Marc Andreessen
http://www.christine.com/15mins/archives/marcand.htm
The Marc Andreessen Interview Page
http://www.dnai.com/~thomst/marca.html
Internet Chronology by Lawrence G. Roberts
http://www.ziplink.net/~lroberts/InternetChronology.html
http://www.Britannica.com

Glossary of Terms

Application: A program that performs a function directly for a user. E-mail is an example of an application.

Chat: To communicate with a person, a group, or a site on the Internet in real time by typing on your keyboard. The words you type appear on the screens of all the other participants in the "chat" and their typing appears on your screen.

Click: To press and immediately release the mouse button. To "click on" something is to position the pointer directly over it and then click.

Browser: A software program that will load and display a web page.

Download: To copy a file from another computer, system or the World Wide Web onto your computer over telephone or cable lines

E-mail: Electronic mail is a system that allows you to send and receive written messages across a network.

FTP: File Transfer Protocol specifies the rules for transferring files from one computer to another.

Hardware: The mechanical components of a computer, such as hard disks, printers, modems, scanners, cards, keyboards and mouse.

HTTP: HyperText Transfer Protocol specifies the rules for communication between World Wide Web servers and browsers.

HyperText: Text that that includes connections, called links, that when clicked on jump the reader to somewhere on another Web page.

Internet: A "super network" that connects many smaller networks around the world together and allows all the computers to exchange information with each other.

Internet Service: A company such as American Online (AOL) that sells access to the Internet to individual customers.

Link: An area of a Web page, usually a word or picture, which you can click on to, to get to another document. Linked words and phrases are usually underlined and often colored.

Mainframe: A type of computer suited for processing vast quantities of information

MIME: Multipurpose Internet Mail Extensions. An extension to Internet e-mail that provides the ability to transfer non-textual data, such as graphics, audio and fax.

Network: A group of computers set up to communicate with one another. The Internet is made up of thousands of individual networks

PC: A personal computer.

Protocol: A set of standardized rules for exchanging information between computers. Different protocols are used for different kinds of communication.

Search Engine: A system that finds World Wide Web pages that contain specific words or phrases. Yahoo.com and hotbot.com are search engines.

Server: A computer program that provides information or services.

Software: Files of a program that tell a computer what to do.

TCP/IP: Transmission Control Protocol/Internet Protocol are the rules computers use to communicate via the Internet. In other words, it is the language shared by all Internet computers.

Unix: A computer operating system first created in Bell Labs during the late1960s. It became popular in the 1970s for general purpose computing, but not on the consumer level. Most Internet hosting is done on Unix machines

Usenet: Usenet is an Internet-accessible computer network that lets people communicate with others by posting and reading articles and opinions about specific subjects, from the environment to 'N Sync in newsgroups. Computers that are connected to Usenet are known as News Servers.

World Wide Web: An interconnected set of hypertext documents located throughout the Internet. The documents are kept on computers called servers, which can send the documents to your computer. It is also frequently called "The Web."

Index